Once upon group ...

Michael and Maggie Kindred

Illustrations by Michael Kindred

4M Publications

4M Publications
10 Station Road, Southwell, Notts. NG25 0ET.
Tel/Ans/Fax: 01636 812883

First published by Southwell Diocesan Education Committee in 1984

Revised edition published by Michael Kindred in 1987
(ISBN 0 9512552 0 7. Revised edition)

New edition published by 4M Publications in 1998

ISBN 0 9530494 2 6. New edition

Printed by Roy Allen Print Ltd., Forest Road, New Ollerton, Newark,
Notts. NG22 9PL

Contents

Introduction

This book is aimed at providing a light-hearted and amusing approach to a subject which can be quite heavy. We hope that it offers an easily digestible way of gaining insights into how groups tick, while at the same time helping to overcome some of the anxieties and doubts which can make people shy away from anything to do with groups and their workings. Even the mention of some of the 'in words' and jargon concerning group behaviour can be enough to put some of us off for life!

Groups are a universal phenomenon. However, the patterns, customs and acceptable content may differ widely in different cultures and races. Group members and facilitators need to bear this in mind when planning and running their groups. The material in this book is written within western white culture and needs adapting to each user group, including people who use manual languages.

Groups are mini-cultures in themselves, and represent all the issues which are present in wider society. It is important, therefore, to try to address some of these issues. For instance, women can be passive in groups, whilst men can unconsciously take the lead. Group leaders should find ways of trying to raise members' awareness. Examples are:
- not making eye contact mainly with men when starting, giving instructions, ending, and during the group life generally;
- when black people are in a minority, it is essential that they are not turned to as 'experts' on race;
- the leader has a responsibility to draw the attention of group members to unconscious racism and other forms of prejudice;
- not using language which assumes that everyone is heterosexual

Throughout the material in this new edition we shall try to make specific points about these issues.

What follows, then, is a brief outline of some aspects of group life in pin-person drawings, annotated with as few words as possible. Remember that behind laughter there may be a grain of truth! Of course, drawings and words are no substitute for the only effective way of learning how groups tick: that is, by belonging to groups of different kinds, either as a member or leader, and by taking part in competently-led courses on group work.

6

Have fun using this book. Take the issues raised seriously, but don't take yourself too seriously.

Michael and Maggie Kindred

Michael Kindred is a freelance games inventor and educational consultant.

Maggie Kindred is a trainer of social work students.
She originally trained as a teacher before moving into social work.

By Michael and Maggie Kindred

> *Once upon a group*
> *Once upon a group Exercises*

By Michael Kindred and Malcolm Goldsmith

> *Communicating with the public*

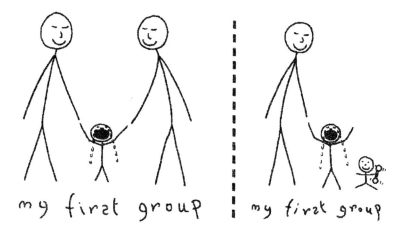

The first group to which most people belong is some kind of family or substitute family.

The ways in which adults and child, or children, get on together - or fail to get on together - affect each member of that family deeply. The ones likely to benefit or suffer most are the children.

The ties and tensions may or may not be more complex where one-parent families are concerned, where substitute parents are involved, or where a child is fostered or adopted.

Our experiences in this first basic family unit will affect how we react and behave in groups to which we belong later on in life.

Think about recent experiences in a group. Were you reacting or behaving or feeling ....

.... a bit like your mother, father or substitute parent used to in a similar situation?

.... a bit like you used to as a child?

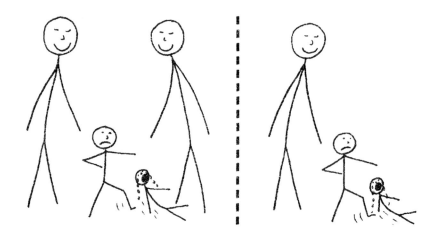

One day, my first group seemed too big

Jealousy directly involves two or more other people. We feel that we want to be included in something which is going on between them, but we are at present excluded. In wanting to 'get in on the act', we may feel like getting rid of the unwanted person or persons in order to make it a cosy 'twosome'.

Envy involves people indirectly. Someone else has a possession, or ability, or attribute which we would like very much, and our feelings get out of proportion.

Think back to times when you were jealous or envious in a group.

Did those feelings have their origins in your early family life?

Some groups may be too large for their purpose

Some people are 'only ones'. Others were born into large families. Some people were the eldest in the family, others were in the middle, some were the youngest. Whatever your position in the family, you would have feelings about it, just as you would have feelings about any increase in the size of your family.

Any such increase would affect how things were done, how present members felt about the new member, and vice versa.

These past experiences may affect how you feel about the size of groups to which you belong now.

Have you been in any groups where 'too many cooks spoiled the broth'?

On the other hand, have you ever wished there were 'many hands to make light work'?

Many groups are too big for the job they have to do.

10

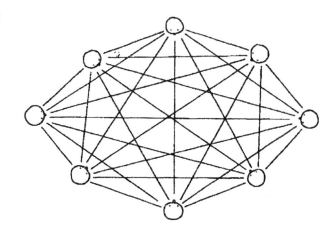

In a group of only 8 people
there are 28 relationships going on at any given time!

Part of the problem for a group which is too big for the job which it has set out to do, is that there are too many relationships going on for comfort. For example, in a family of parent, parent and child, the relationships which are going on are between:

parent and parent   parent and child   parent and child

If another child is born into the family, the number of relationships increase to those between:

parent and parent   parent and older child
parent and younger child   parent and older child
parent and younger child   older child and younger child

Add one to a group of three and the number of relationships with which members have to deal has doubled.

Formula for working out   (number in group) x (number in group minus one)
how many relationships are going on: ──
                                                              2

Therefore in a class of 30 children plus a teacher, the number of relationships is $\frac{31 \times 30}{2} = 465$ (!)

Members should be clear about the main purpose of the group

Think about various groups to which you have belonged. In each one, did the leader .....

..... state clearly its purpose in the written or spoken invitation to join?

..... give members the opportunity, at the first meeting, so say what their expectations were?

..... offer the chance to see whether or not these expectations were realistic?

..... discuss with members whether or not they understood the purpose of the group, and whether or not they agreed with it?

..... make opportunities during the life of the group for evaluation of how the purpose was being fulfilled?

The more times you answer 'No' to the above, the higher the likelihood of genuine discontent in a group.

Not everyone likes marathons

Have you ever been put off by the number of meetings planned for a group?

Perhaps you have gone to the first few sessions and then realised that a certain crispness is lacking and that the task has been spread over far too long a time.

There is, of course, the other side of the coin. Have you sometimes felt that too much was being crammed into the time allotted?

The number of sessions planned for a group needs to be in keeping with the task to be accomplished.

Where you meet is important.

Neutral territories are sometimes best. If you meet in one particular member's house all the time, you may find a few jealousies or resentments creeping in.

We imagine that you have been in groups which have gone badly while meeting in the best of rooms.

On the other hand, you have probably met in the most unwelcoming of places, and yet been thrilled by what happened in the group.

It depends to a large extent on the members.

However, what the meeting place is like usually matters more than people think. Warmth, comfort, acceptable lighting level, adequate space, are all important. Suitable access is crucial, including physical considerations such as the number of steps from the outside to the room. Audibility within the room needs to be checked out. Think also about other kinds of access: times when children need to be collected from school, and festival days for the major religions. The timing can only be set with the specific members in mind.

If possible, it's not a bad idea
to have similar kinds of chairs for everybody

There are, of course, situations where this is difficult, such as when meeting in someone's home. It is important to realise that some people may need a chair of a certain kind due to difficulties such as backache or arthritis - this does not negate the 'similar chairs' principle.

If all the chairs are not the same, you need to be aware of how certain kinds of chairs can influence the contribution of the occupants. For example .....

..... someone who has cornered the only armchair, when everyone else is on hardback chairs, may use it to opt out of the proceedings quietly, or to feel somewhat superior, or to take a smug as well as a snug view of the proceedings.

..... someone on a stool may feel left out, and, literally, on edge!

The kind of chair used is important, although often it's Hobson's Choice. One of us once went to meeting held in a school for infants, where we were all sitting on incredibly small chairs for a very long time. It could have been described as an overflow meeting! No-one has perfect conditions. Telling people to bring a cushion has been an essential ingredient in 'joining instructions' for some courses.

How the chairs are arranged *does* matter!

Have you been in small groups where the chairs were arranged so that you couldn't see everybody's face?

Have you been in larger groups and meetings where you could see mostly backs of necks?

In either case, how far did you feel part of what was happening?

How many times have you chosen to sit on the back row if you were not all that interested in going in the first place?

In particular, don't sit on top of each other

Holy (or unholy) huddles can frighten the life out of someone who likes a bit of space to themselves.

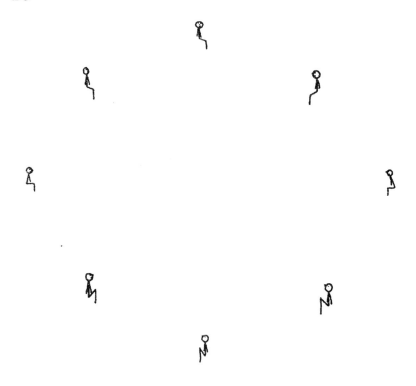

People need physical space as well as emotional space

Have you ever felt that you were sitting too close together in a group?

Or too far apart?

What is too close for you may not be close enough for someone else!

It is interesting to see the ways in which people knowingly or unknowingly adjust the space between themselves and those next to them.

Think about groups to which you have belonged. How would you have spaced the chairs?

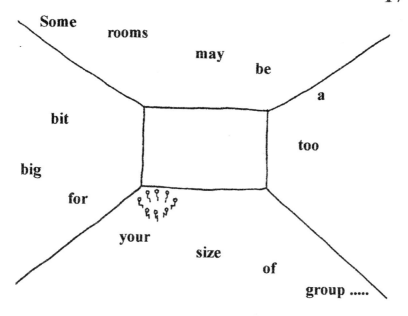

Some rooms may be a bit big too for your size of group .....

..... ontheotherhand theycouldbetoosmall

Have you ever met as the only group in one corner of a large hall?

Some people can feel quite lost in that sort of situation.

Or have you suffered from claustrophobia and realised that feeling included has its limits?

The size of the place chosen for a meeting can affect the working of the group to some degree.

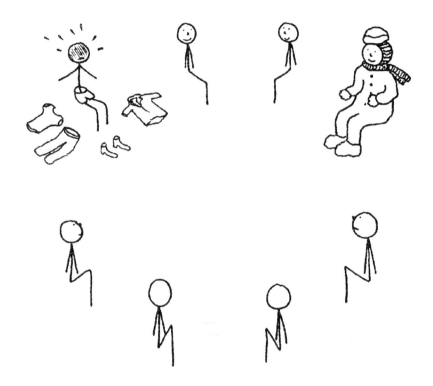

**Getting the right temperature for the room
is important .... it may also be difficult!**

The meeting place may be at an agreeable temperature at the beginning.

But meetings warm up - physically as well as emotionally - as the meeting proceeds.

Have you ever been in groups where the leader checked occasionally that the room was agreeably warm for everyone?

There are other ways of getting some oxygen!

Ventilating a room to suit all tastes can sometimes be a problem. Some outdoor types would probably like to fling all the doors and windows wide open, while others may feel like fitting draught excluders strips during the coffee break.

A healthy stream of fresh air through an open window can turn one person's position into pneumonia corner. On the other hand the 'sealed capsule' syndrome can turn some members a whiter shade of pale.

Perhaps you have welcomed those times where the leader 'aired' the problem, so to speak, and tried to help everyone to feel reasonably comfortable.

This point may seem laboured: we believe that attention to basic physical needs symbolises a concern for the less tangible needs and gives a powerful message that the leaders care about such things.

Is the level of lighting more suited to interrogations or developing films?

How often have you been in groups where the level of lighting has been given little consideration by the organisers or leaders?

It is something which deserves more attention that it usually gets.

The level of lighting can create moods and atmospheres ranging from restful, to seductive, to dramatic, to intense. Our experiences in groups can be enhanced if we get the lighting as good as we can make it.

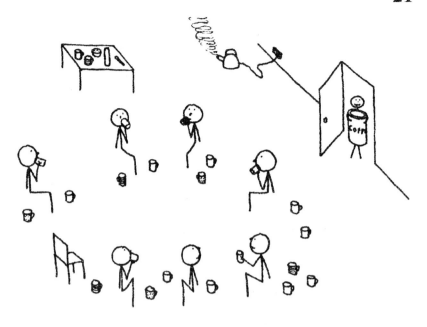

If you decide to have a coffee break, make sure it doesn't go on too long

You have probably found it helpful when you have been offered one or more short breaks (depending on the length of the meeting).

Such breaks, one of which may include refreshments, give everyone a legitimate chance to stretch, yawn and change position as necessary.

Also the attention span of most people is less than we imagine. It is worth timing the breaks carefully: at the beginning a drink is welcoming but can postpone the getting down to work. Any break disrupts the flow. Some leaders wait for the 'right moment'. Others, ourselves included, feel this never comes, and that it is better to know in advance when the refreshments are going to arrive, and to organise the work around that timing.

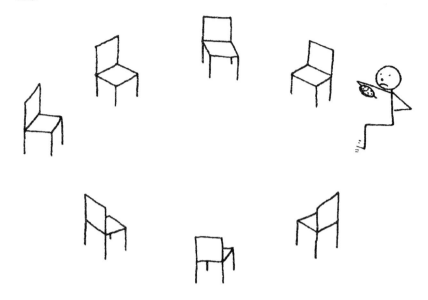

It is helpful if the group starts on time

It can be frustrating, for those who have taken care to arrive on time, to wait for others who are late.

Some people are, of course, unavoidably late at times.

Therefore, it is important that groups or meetings start at the time stated, or else the number of latecomers is likely to increase, and dissatisfaction will grow among those who continue to arrive on time.

However uncomfortable it may seem, it is generally better to welcome the late person by non-verbal communication and a brief word, than by attempting to recapitulate, which can be done more easily later.

Some people, realising that they are late, may find it very difficult to knock and enter. They are usually helped by the kind of welcome mentioned above - knowing that they can come in with a minimum of fuss.

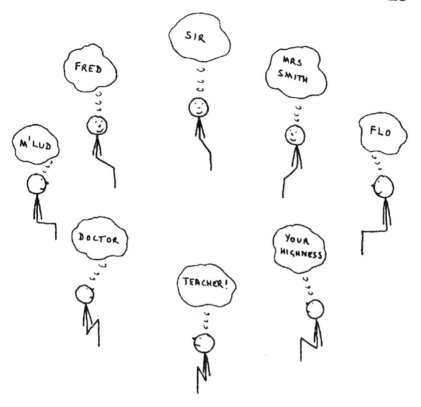

How would you like people to refer to you in the group?

Have you been in a group where you have been addressed in a way which made you feel slightly uncomfortable or embarrassed?

It is helpful for people to have the chance to say how they would like to be known.

Never shorten names because you find them difficult to pronounce. This applies particularly to unusual and 'non-English' names. Permission needs to be sought for the use of first names - don't assume this - check first.

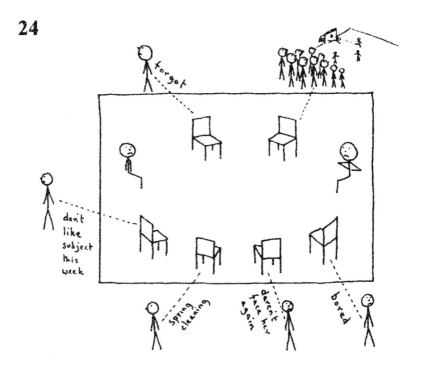

Groups work best if the membership is stable

If you say that you are going to join a group which is to have a series of meetings, it is important that you take this commitment seriously.

Nothing is more dispiriting to the leader and the regular members than spasmodic attendance.

There are some kinds of groups which, by their very nature, generate attendance which varies from meeting to meeting. Support groups and committees often fall into this category. The leader and members should take steps to use this kind of group as positively as possible, and people should not be made to feel guilty about irregular attendance. Extra attention needs to be given each time to re-stating ground rules, introductions and endings. In this sort of group, each individual meeting covers the full range of group phenomena.

It is important, at the start of a group, to discuss the matter of confidentiality

The degree of confidentiality will vary according to the type of group.

A group which meets to help members with their personal problems will demand a very high degree of confidentiality.

Unless members feel that safeguard, how will they be able to share some of what is troubling them?

Some leaders fail to find an adequate consultant who is outside the group. They can then find themselves needing to talk to inappropriate people for support. It is amazing how such conversations return to their source, with unhelpful consequences.

Limits to confidentiality need to be stated, eg: 'If anyone in the group reveals serious harm to another person which they have not shared until now, this may have to be taken outside the group.'

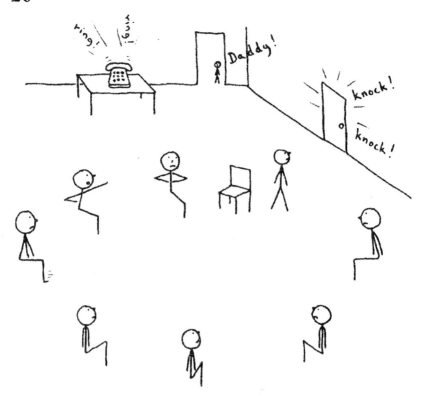

Sometimes there may be the odd interruption

Have you had experiences where the leader of a group has constantly broken off to answer the door or phone or deal with a family problem?

Did you feel that he or she was not really interested in the group and what it was doing?

The more committed everyone is will be in proportion to the productivity of the group. If someone leaves the room because of distress or a need for space, other members should follow *only* if it is considered that there is a serious risk to that person's well-being.

You may find it helpful
to have a few boundaries and limits defined

These boundaries and limits apply to what people do *in* the group - what they do outside the group is their own affair.

Sometimes people's personal agendas need to be looked at. A personal agenda is that which a person knowingly or unknowingly brings to a group from his/her recent or past life outside the group, and which to a greater or lesser degree gets in the way of what the group as a whole is supposed to be doing. We all have personal agendas and with a little insight and help we can make sure that their effect on the life of the group is minimal.

If there seem to be particular personal agendas which are affecting the life of the group, there should be some encouragement from the leader for these to be acknowledged and discussed so that their effect on the group is minimised.

It is worth mentioning that, especially in discussion-type groups, some members will stray from the straight and narrow and talk about anything but the subject in hand. Leaders can sometimes have a hard job in keeping them to the point. Those who have come to the meeting understanding its purpose and are trying to fulfil it, may feel annoyed and frustrated.

'Er ... er ... does anyone mind if I don't smoke?'

The question of whether or not members may smoke should be dealt with in the publicity prior to the formation of the group, or at its first meeting.

Some non-smokers find it quite difficult to respond honestly to someone asking 'Do you mind if I smoke?' and may say 'No.' in order to avoid having to cope with potentially uncomfortable feelings.

This can lead to suppressed resentment and can hinder the development of helpful relationships.

On the other hand, some smokers find it equally difficult to ask if they may smoke, knowing that some people don't like smoky atmospheres, and they too may sit through sessions with a growing resentment.

Either way, it is good to air (!) the subject at the beginning.

Many buildings now have an automatic non-smoking rule - it is becoming easier for private houses to follow suit, and for group leaders to suggest where people may smoke, eg: garden or workshop.

It is helpful to finish sessions on time

An important aspect of 'boundaries' is concerned with beginning and ending sessions.

Nothing is more annoying to most people than meetings which go on and on past their allotted finishing time. Some meetings don't even have a stated finishing time, and this can create difficulties for people who like to know how much time they are committing.

Finishing meetings on time helps to prevent boredom, yawns, rebellions, walk-outs and reducing membership. Bringing up important issues at the last minute is a well-known phenomenon which can make meetings drag on beyond their allotted time - see page 69.

Task v Maintenance

Everything which takes place in a group is referred to as the process.

This process comprises two distinct but interdependent functions: task and maintenance.

The task is that which the group has come together to achieve.

Maintenance is the building up and nurturing of the relationships between all members of the group.

If the task is concentrated upon at the expense of maintaining relationships in the group, then the co-operation necessary for completing the task will deteriorate, and so it will not be completed satisfactorily.

If the maintenance of relationships is concentrated on at the expense of the task, the completion of the task suffers setbacks.

Therefore it follows that task and maintenance need to go hand in hand, and although the degree to which either is attended to at any given time will vary, they should always be complementary to each other.

Common threads running through various theories and models of group life

There are various theories and models of how a group develops during its life. A brief outline follows of what seems fairly common to all these, showing that three basic phenomena tend to occur and recur.

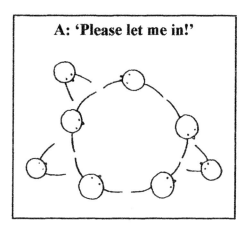

A: 'Please let me in!'

At the beginning of the group life, members feel it is important to establish their position. The natural desire to feel needed and accepted and included is very prominent, although different members will show these desires in different ways.

B: 'The winner!'

At one or more points during the group life there will be bids for control, often directed at the designated leadership. Those doing the bidding will adopt different ways of trying to establish who is in control, varying from an open and frank attack on, or defence of, the designated leader, to more subtle ploys such as quietly manipulating others into liking the way they perform in the group!

C: Affection and disaffection

As the group progresses, members demonstrate different kinds of feelings for each other. Feelings between any two members can alter during the life of the group, so that what started out as antagonism could turn into affection, or vice versa.

These three phenomena ...

    A: needing to feel accepted

    B: the desire for control

    C: developing feelings about other members
        and commitment to the task

        ... continue to appear in varying proportions during the life of a group, even though at different stages one may seem more apparent than the other two.

Some groups are more creative than others!

What things give life to a group, invest it with a vital spark, make it tick? There are many, but one major factor is the degree of creativity among its members. This creativity is closely linked to the ability to play, which arises and develops in childhood - and very often is stifled later on by the stresses and pressures of adult life.

Think back to the world of the young. Children love to ask lots of questions, they are curious and want to experiment. They love to play not only with toys, but with odds and ends, and make things out of them. They have a rich fantasy life and a fertile imagination. They have a sense of wonder and delight in exploring the world around them. They have fun. This may describe the world of childhood for the fortunate ones. The less fortunate who experience poor socio-economic conditions and ill health may be deprived of many of these opportunities to grow into a well-balanced adult. Even so, in such circumstances, 'necessity may be the mother of invention'. It is also worth considering that the 'fortunate' children may lose some opportunities for creativity by having ready-made toys and materials.

The more members of a group are in touch with the positive aspects of childhood outlined above, the more they will contribute to a group life which is lively and fun.

Some people who are anxious about being in a group may prefer the seat nearest the door

If you are one of the first to walk into the room where the group is meeting, how do you choose your seat .....

..... next to the leader (if he or she is already seated)?
    Does this give you a feeling of kinship with the leader?
    Does it make you feel more secure and allay some of
       your anxieties?

..... opposite the leader? Do you need to make sure you can see him/her?
    Are you preparing to do battle?

..... nearest the door? Do you favour flight instead of fight? Do you need
    to leave early?

Do you find it difficult to take the last seat if everyone has arrived before you?

There are other ways of introducing a subject

How many times have you been in groups where the subject matter was introduced by a straight talk from notes? Perhaps you would have been more interested if one of the following had been used:

- slides and/or a tape
- role play - eg: where members are given a particular situation and asked to act out how they would respond to it
- learning exercise - eg: where members are asked to perform a particular task, and then helped to discuss how and what they had learned
- educational game - eg: a game like Monopoly can be played and people are asked afterwards what criteria they used to make decisions, and how they felt about other players
- quiz
- passage from a book
- reaction to pictures and advertisements
- simulation - eg: players enter into situations such as trading, setting up a workplace, producing a newspaper, and so on, and discuss at the end how they reacted to other players, and to what was required of them during the simulation

Be aware that many highly intelligent people have reading difficulties or are dyslexic. Make exercises tactile as well as based on words.

36

If you dive in with a big splash straight away, the leader may throw the odd lifebelt, but you have to learn to swim

Anxiety is usually largely responsible for the way in which some people make a contribution in the opening sessions of a group. They 'dive right in' and say things which they may regret later on. It is usually difficult for them to go back on what they said - they are afraid of losing face.

Personality will also have some bearing on how and when we contribute to a group. For example, extroverts will be more likely to say the first thing that comes into their head. They will also be more likely to change their minds quickly in the light of new information, once again running the risk of diving in and creating a splash. Someone who is more introverted will tend to reflect on things before saying anything. Introverts, of course, run the risk of being considered uninterested, or indecisive and others may wonder what they are thinking. This is not to say that one way of contributing is right and another wrong - it is saying that it is helpful to be aware of how personality affects the ways in which people contribute to the group process.

A competent leader may be able to help 'divers' through the difficulties to some extent, but the person concerned has to take responsibility for the splash!

**People find different ways
of not communicating with each other**

Various things happen in the relationships within a group which cause breakdowns in communication.

The signs of these breakdowns vary from the very obvious to those which could go unnoticed.

Someone may deliberately ignore what another person is saying, and almost interrupt them, changing the subject at the same time.

Another person may be upset by what has just happened between themselves and another member, and avoid eye contact for the rest of the session.

Whatever the signs are, it is useful to be able to spot them, because we may be able to help someone who has received the worst of an 'exchange' and is feeling somewhat defeated, or hurt - or just plain angry.

38

Sometimes, communication in a group
may be of the non-verbal kind!

Roughly 90% of all face-to-face communication is non-verbal. We are so used to communicating by words, spoken or printed, that we sometimes forget that a great deal of what we communicate to others is done through:

- facial expression
- posture
- gestures (specific movements of fingers, hands and arms)
- skin (blushing, sweating)
- smiles and laughter
- crying

It is sad that most of us are not very good at listening to what others are saying - we are usually more interested in what *we* want to say.

It is important to note that the same gesture may have one meaning in one culture and a different one in another. Think carefully before commenting on someone's gestures or posture. A simple example is the use of eye contact, which in some cultures means lack of respect or confrontation. So, looking down may denote respect rather than hesitancy or avoidance.

When it comes to being aware of the things which are not being put into words, most of us could do with developing such skills.

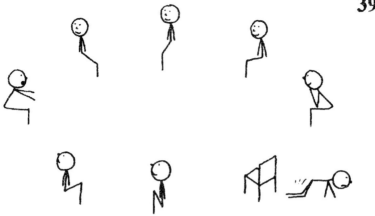

Be sensitive to anyone
who may be opting out almost unnoticed

Some people may become so anxious, threatened or frightened by what is happening in a group that they find ways of opting out.

They may remain unusually silent for long periods. They may even leave the room - this is often a cry for help or attention rather than a real wish to leave.

They may twist in their chair so as to try not to look at the group, or at a specific member of the group.

They may engage in 'pairing', ie: finding a mate in the group to whom they constantly refer for support, so that they feel safer.

They may make a lot of jokes about what is going on in an attempt to defuse a threatening situation.

A good leader will notice these signs and will try to help the person to feel a welcome part of the group again.

Silence, however, can mean thoughtful consideration. If there is a lot of silence, the leader should try asking what the quality of the silence is - this will open up the situation.

Be sensitive to other people's feelings

In your anxiety to cope with your own feelings, you may at times ride roughshod over other people's. Try to remember that every member of the group has his or her vulnerable areas, a tenderness which, once hurt, may take some time to heal.

So, what does it mean to be strong? Does it mean enforcing your will on others, keeping a stiff upper lip, bottling things up?

What does it mean to be weak? Does it mean sharing the fact that you are afraid of speaking in groups. that you are worried about being 'sat upon', that you find authority figures daunting?

What a lot of people count as strength is usually only a show of power used to cover up deeper insecurity.

What a lot of people count as weakness is usually evidence of the humanity that we all share - how prone we are to make mistakes, to get things wrong, to fail to see what is in front of our noses! Admitting some of these things is normally a sign of strength and depth of character.

The paradox is that your strength may lie in behaving and reacting in a way which apparently strong people would dismiss as being weak!

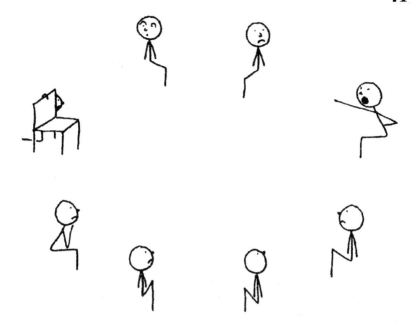

Some people are very honest when it comes to feelings
- other people's, of course!

Try to imagine what you are about to say to someone in the group, being said by them to you.

How would you feel?

If you think you would feel all right, have you had more help than they may have had in developing insight into understanding oneself and others?

If you don't know, or aren't sure, then err on the safe side!

Start sentences with 'I think ...', 'I feel ...' and make sure that you *don't* speak for others. Asking everyone to do the same can be a very useful ground rule at the beginning. The leader will usually have to feed in a few reminders from time to time!

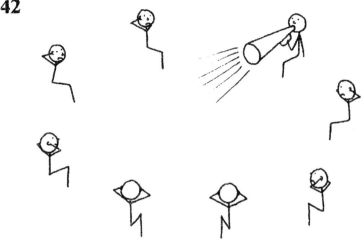

The art of listening
may also apply to what is not being said

A child once defined 'listening' as 'wanting to hear'.

There is an art to listening. It involves really wanting to hear what another person is saying.

There is also an art to 'listening between the lines', to pick up what is not being said.

Listening means more than just saying 'Yes' and 'No' in the right places.

Posture and gesture and facial expression can convey whether we are really listening or not.

We are usually so busy working out what we want to say, that we wait impatiently for someone else to finish so that we can 'put our spoke in'.

If you are not sure what someone is really saying, then use the counselling technique of checking: 'I think I heard you saying .... is that what you meant?'

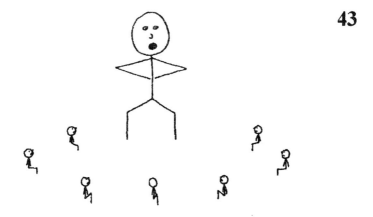

**Some people (only occasionally of course!)
can be a trifle dominant**

A person who is unsure of himself or herself and feels insecure, may deal with these feelings in a variety of ways.

One way is to try to dominate others in order to feel less threatened by them and feel safer.

If a person is allowed to dominate the group, various things can happen: people will leave, the leader will lose co-operation from other members, the dominant person will take over the leadership, a rebellion may emerge when a few members of the group band together to 'sit on' the dominant one.

It is better if any tendency to dominate is dealt with when it is recognised.

It is helpful to deal with threatening emotions earlier rather than later.

The leader should work towards encouraging others members to help dominant personalities to take a back seat sometimes.

It is unhelpful for the leader continually to be acting as a controller while others enjoy the show and take no responsibility. He/she can pass the responsibility on by pointing out that the group seems to be expecting him/her to be a referee!

Fight or flight (or freeze?)

Most of us find it difficult to experience emotions *and* give ourselves time to decide whether or not we need to act upon them. Usually, the stronger the emotion, the greater the urge to act.

One example of this comes in what is generally referred to as the fight or flight response. It is very basic and necessary in the animal kingdom, and it is good that it is part of human nature too, but all to often it appears in inappropriately large doses in our relationships.

If someone in the group takes a tilt at us, do we rise up in anger and charge straight into battle, or do we turn on our heels and run like mad? Or are we rooted to the spot, frozen with fear?

Is either course really necessary if we think about it? Would it be possible to *tell* someone how their behaviour makes us feel, without *acting* upon those feelings? For example, would it be possible to tell another member of the group that they were making you feel like hitting them, and why this was so? In this way, you are at least offering the chance of opening up some kind of dialogue, which if taken can lead to a building-up of a relationship rather than a breaking down or abandoning of it. If the offer is declined, you are the one who has shown some insight and inner strength. It is always more helpful to describe how another's behaviour is making *us* feel, rather than condemning that behaviour. The rule about starting sentences with 'I' (p41) applies here.

Some group leaders are occasionally
less democratic than they might be

If a group leader comes over as rather autocratic at times, reactions from members will vary.

Some people enjoy being told what to do or think, and a relationship similar to that between a parent and child (appropriate enough in that setting) is maintained in an immature way between two adults, thus allowing little chance for personal growth.

Some people do not enjoy being told what to do or think, due to their previous life experiences. Rebellions against the leadership will almost surely develop.

Most of us fall somewhere between these two, and may find ourselves alternating in feelings about the leadership. This part of the 'control' dynamic is described on p37.

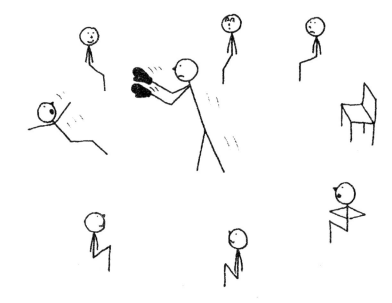

Sometimes there may be a bid for the leadership

If someone has set himself or herself up as a leader, then you can be sure that someone else will want to knock them down.

If a group is meeting regularly over a period, the leadership may remain uncontested for a while (sometimes called the 'honeymoon period'), but after that, other people may begin to feel that they could do a better job.

A competent leader will recognise these bids, and bring them out into the open to be discussed and, hopefully, resolved.

If the bids are ignored, then trouble is in store, because members of the group will begin to take sides and the real purpose of the group will be in danger of being sidelined.

Once control issues have been resolved for a time, the group enters a creative period. It is normal for control issues to re-emerge towards the end.

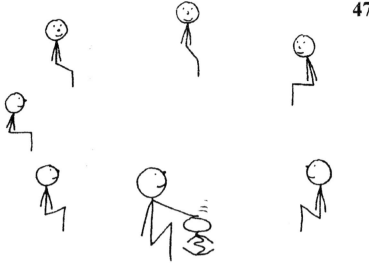

Co-leadership is not always easy!

Have you been part of a group where, instead of just one leader, there have been two?

If they haven't spent a lot of time beforehand preparing how they are going to work with each other, and getting to know each other quite well, then the group will suffer.

For example, did noticeable differences of opinion emerge between them as to how the group should be run at different stages?

Did one co-leader try to wrench all the leadership for himself or herself? Did the other respond by doing battle, or by giving up and becoming to all intents and purposes an aggrieved member of the group?

Notice how co-leadership is handled if there is a man/woman team. Have the pair conformed to society's stereotypes, or have they made efforts to reverse these? How is the whole group working on this? Do the women always make the refreshments, the men act as recorders and presenters, or are such tasks shared?

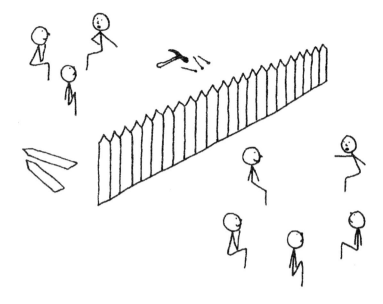

Sub-groups can form

When two or three people begin to disagree with the leader, and with others who appear to be positive about the leadership, then the group will fail to remain a single unit working together for a purpose, and will become two separate groups within the group.

As with bids for the leadership, if this sub-grouping is not acknowledged and dealt with, the effectiveness of the group is at risk if it is a task centred group with a job to do. If the group is using the time specifically for studying itself, a simple 'mirror' comment about what is going on may be the best remedy, eg: 'I notice that there are several conversations going on at this point.'

Sub-groups tend to represent the wider society, eg: men/women, racial groups, gay and heterosexual people. At times, it can be useful to use these positively, eg: the women and men to work in separate sub-groups for a time. The support gained from this benefits the whole group when the results are shared.

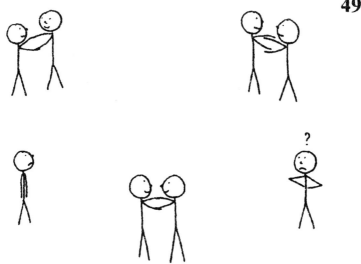

What is known as pairing
can make some people feel left out

If two people (or more) start sitting together at each session, and exchanging nods, winks or whispering confidences, then this can irritate others or make them feel jealous and left out.

To make up for these feelings, other pairings can start.

The group is then on the way to disintegration in much the same way as when a sub-group has formed (see previous page)

The leader should bring the pairing out into the open and help members to look at the reasons for it, and the effect it is having on the group.

As a phenomenon, it may be a sign of insecurity, non-commitment to the group and its task, or the need to feel more in control/ be heard/ have more influence. Check whether there are enough ways of ensuring everyone's view is given equal weight. A useful device is a round, ie: asking everyone in turn to state briefly their view or current feelings.

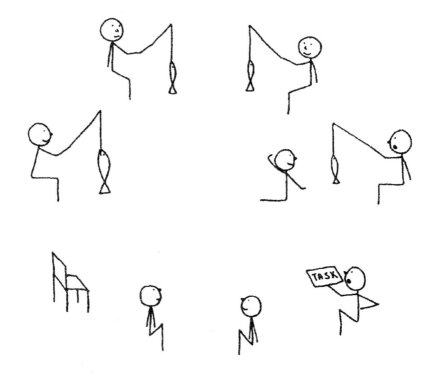

Red herrings

At times, due to fear, enthusiasm, insecurity, rebelliousness, happiness and so on, most of us knowingly or unknowingly deflect other members of the group from the task in hand. Some people are more accomplished deflectors than others, but we all do it to some degree: the anecdote that suddenly occurs to us, the need to change the subject quickly to avoid the 'hot potato', the story about what happened to someone outside the group, instead of what is happening to us right now.

The odd red herring here and there can be acceptable, especially if the group can be helped to see why such a deflection was used. A whole shoal unacknowledged could break the group net!

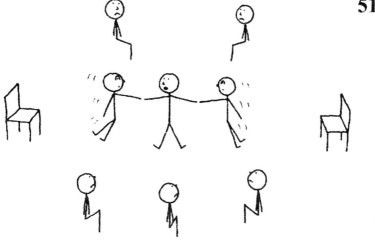

Some people get too involved

We all get involved in different ways and at different levels with any group to which we belong. The involvement can be practical, intellectual, emotional or spiritual - in any combination.

It will vary at different stages during the life of the group. Sometimes it will vary almost from minute to minute.

The reasons for getting involved are numerous - they include:

- interest
- excitement
- curiosity
- some emotional need not met outside the group
- pressure from one or more other members of the group
- some unrecognised need which is not being met

It is difficult to say what getting too involved means - it will vary from person to person. An example of over-involvement which could lead to problems would be that of a group member continually wishing to focus on what he/she sees as other members' difficulties.

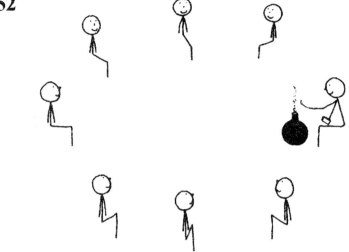

There are those of us who can be quietly subversive

The rebellious toddler and the cantankerous adolescent lurk around in all of us!

When we take a tilt at authority or people we don't like, we can find it quite exciting and fun - it may not be so enjoyable for those on the receiving end.

Sometimes people will steer a course between being openly rebellious or 'awkward', and saying nothing, thereby probably bottling up their feelings. The subversion may emerge as a sort of 'borderline' remark where it is hard to decide whether they are being quietly rebellious, or whether they have put their finger on something important which is happening in the group which needs talking about.

It is worth noting that subversive behaviour can mask as constructive comment. Note carefully the kind of questions which are asked - are they a disguised way of catching the leader out?

Some groups/leaders may, of course, need to be challenged!

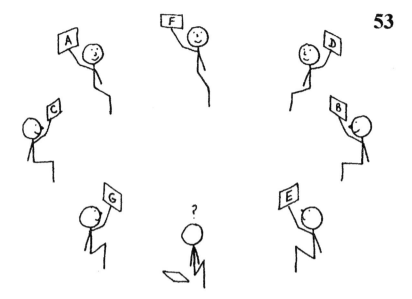

There may be odd times when it's difficult to reach a decision

Someone once said that democracy is the least evil form of government.

On the one hand it gives everyone a chance to influence the way the decision-making goes. On the other hand, it can lead to a watered-down form of what might have been a very creative idea.

In groups, it is important continually to evaluate the degree to which people feel free to contribute to the decision-making processes. Is anyone feeling pushed out or ignored. Is anyone's opinion lightly dismissed without good reason? Is there a good level of co-operation in the group?

Note that truly consensual decision-making takes a long time. For some decisions another form of decision-making process is better, eg: a sub-group of members who have some expertise works separately and brings recommendations to the whole group for ratification. A type of situation which needs autocratic decision-making occurs when a fire alarm goes off!

'Please, sir'

All groups, like families, have their own rules, often not stated, but nevertheless very powerful. These are known as the group norms.

Have you noticed, in groups to which you have belonged, what rules were being adhered to? Did the leader help members to be aware of what these were and try to ensure that individual's rights were not being trampled upon?

A good exercise is to ask the group to write down what they think the unwritten rules are, once the group has had enough time together for these to evolve. You may gain some surprising insights into what is really going on!

Sometimes someone may erect the odd barrier

Right from birth, we put up all sorts of emotional defences and barriers to help us cope with what makes us feel insecure, frightened, threatened, anxious, worried.

Sometimes, the situation which has threatened us initially, is repeated enough times for the defence to become a really hardened one.

For example, perhaps you couldn't cope with your parent's anger - so now you tend to 'pour oil on troubled waters' and 'make the peace' in any situations involving confrontation, so that other people's anger is kept under, and so that your own doesn't surface.

You may, for instance, find yourself 'keeping a stiff upper lip', having a 'poker face', denying that you feel in a certain way about something when challenged.

Contrary to popular opinion, competent leaders do not rush at people to 'break them down'. They recognise each individual's need for these barriers and try to find ways of making people more comfortable.

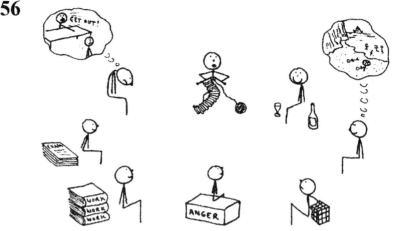

The hidden agenda

There are always things in people's lives outside the group which affect their contribution in the group. This is known as the hidden agenda. Sometimes it's not so hidden!

You take your emotional suitcase wherever you go. Some people keep their suitcases tightly locked, others let them spill all over the place. Most of us get a few things out from time to time, putting some back hastily - others the group may help us to wear for a time.

Things which have happened to us an hour ago, that day, that week, five years ago, in childhood, or things which are in the future such as a wedding, holidays, a difficult meeting, and so on, can be on our minds while the set agenda for the session is being worked through.

Some of these experiences may be positive, but some will have been upsetting enough to get in the way of our effective contribution to the work of the group.

That's not a criticism implying that we shouldn't let them get in the way - it is saying that we should acknowledge that this is normal for all of us, and should be recognised as such.

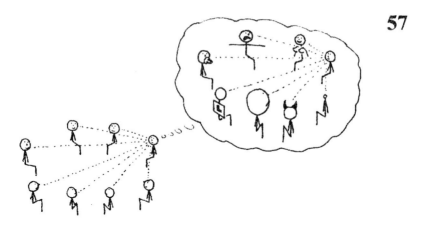

How do we see other members of the group?
We may project aspects of our personality onto them

If I am 'big-headed' but am not aware of it, I can easily think of someone else as big-headed. I then don't have to consider whether I may have the fault of which I accuse others.

If I know that I have a cruel streak in me, and I wish that I hadn't, and don't want other people to know, it is easy for me to accuse other people of being cruel. It lets me off the hook. It makes my own cruel streak seem not so bad if others are cruel too.

These kinds of 'projections' of aspects of our personality onto others, go on in different degrees all the time in any group.

Of course, it may be the other way round. In a group we may be under pressure to accept too readily others' views of us. The leader needs to watch for members' discomfort if this seems to be happening, as unreservedly taking in everything which people say about us, is unhelpful.

If projections and the feelings associated with them are gradually acknowledged, and people make a genuine attempt to understand them, then relationships can improve. If they remain unacknowledged, relationships will continue at a shallow level and any work the group has to do will suffer accordingly.

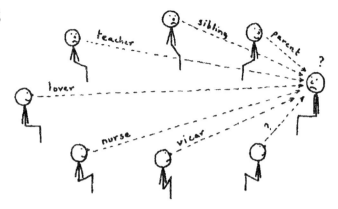

Anyone may transfer feelings associated with someone they know outside the group, to another member,

This can be confusing, as lots of transferences can be taking place at any given moment.

Someone in the group may see you as the 'spitting image' of someone they know. Or you may have a particular characteristic, mannerism or type of voice, which reminds them very much of someone they know (or knew).

If the person they are reminded of is/was 'lovely' or 'fatherly/motherly' or '*so* kind' in their eyes, you may find they are seeing the same qualities in you.

If the person they are reminded of is/was someone they 'couldn't stand at any price', you may find that you are being ostracised by them, and it's no fault of yours.

The most common 'transference' concerns a person's parent(s). If, for example, a person really loved their mother, and you remind them very much of their mother, you may find them more than usually affectionate towards you. The reverse is also true - transference often occurs in a negative way if aspects of our early relationships were difficult. Many transference phenomena in groups come from experience in school - we have all spent a large part of our vulnerable years there. A simple exercise, 'Past experiences in groups', helps people to recognise some of the 'luggage' they are bringing.

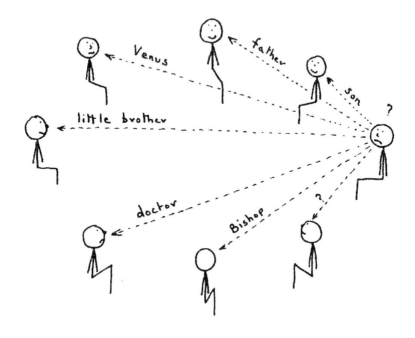

What feelings associated with people outside the group are you transferring to other members in the group?

If other people are transferring things to you, what are you doing to them?

If you were afraid of a parent, for example, and someone in the group has an irritating mannerism just like your parent's, you may find yourself becoming afraid of that member of the group.

If these transferences can gradually be acknowledged, there is a real chance that misunderstandings can be resolved to some extent, paving the way for deeper relationships within the group.

It can be quite helpful to become more aware of the qualities you put on to others which belong to significant people in your life, particularly parents.

60

Why do we need someone to be the scapegoat?

If you find difficulties are entering into a relationship, or you feel that life is difficult at present, it is easier to blame other people or circumstances, than to take any responsibility yourself.

It is so easy to see the problems of life as being 'out there', and that the difficulties are caused by other people.

Of course, other people can cause us pain or anxiety and circumstances can be hard.

But that doesn't necessarily let us off the hook. We need to look at what part we are playing in a deteriorating relationship. Which problems are of our own making?

In groups, it is very easy to get another, perhaps apparently 'weaker' member of the group, to take the blame. They become the scapegoat for group problems which are not of their making, or may be only partly so.

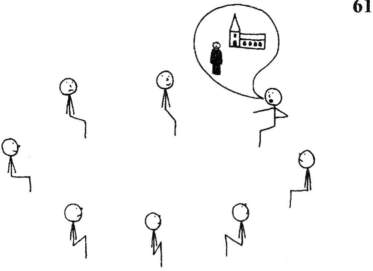

For safety, the scapegoat
is sometimes located outside the group

Rather than find someone in the group to blame for the group's own short-comings, it is much less threatening to blame someone or some 'body' outside the group. Likely candidates are:

- the system
- the management
- religious leaders
- the state
- society
- the government
- teachers
- doctors
- the youth of today
- God

A competent leader will be aware of this 'running away' and will bring the focus of attention back into the group.

The group casualty

Have you found that sometimes one or two members of the group will initiate and encourage a 'case conference' about another member of the group who has shown some anxiety or fear or difficulty?

Soon, if the leader is not careful, everyone will become hooked on this golden opportunity to forget their own problems or the task of the group.

Have you ever come under the microscope in this way? If so, how did it feel?

Some may find the sudden attention flattering initially and join in the game eagerly. Eventually, the pace may hot up as the probes go deeper, and suddenly the 'patient' may be desperate to locate the EXIT sign. Others may immediately resent the appearance of 'doctors and nurses' who didn't seem to be there before. Either way, it is usually a harrowing experience for the one who is the centre of this kind of attention.

Labelling people causes problems

A convenient way of avoiding facing up to problems - our own and other people's - is to label or stereotype them.

If we can give a name to someone's upsetting or worrying behaviour, then it somehow seems safer; we may even be misled into thinking we have solved the matter.

It is much harder to avoid labelling people and treat them as fallible human beings like ourselves.

So, in groups, where feelings of insecurity can run quite high, labelling is an easy escape from trying to discover what is really hindering the growth of a relationship.

Labelling is particularly destructive in the use of language towards black people, people with disability, gay and lesbian people, older people, and minority groups generally. The group needs to work out a way of trying to change language which anyone finds offensive.

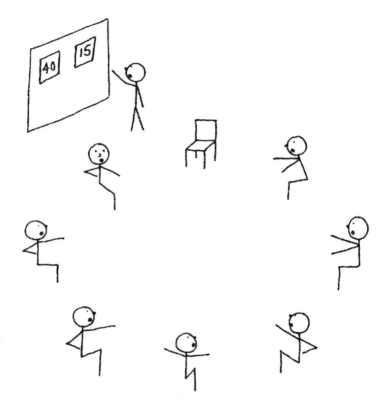

If you want to score points off each other ...

If you are feeling somewhat at a disadvantage in a group for some reason, one way of trying to cope is to do or say something which puts another member (or members) at a disadvantage.

For example, someone may have disagreed with something you said. You then wait for a chance to disagree with them.

This game of 'point scoring' can easily start in a group, and unless it is acknowledged and talked through, it can disrupt the real task of the group.

kite

hobby
horse

soap box

Arrangements may have to be made for the disposal of equipment which is cluttering up the group space

We all have our favourite topics, opinions we love to give other people the benefit of, 'pearls of wisdom' that people are just waiting to hear drop from our lips, and so on.

Irrespective of what the group is supposed to be doing, some people are itching to hold the floor and work the discussion round to themselves.

They need to be steered, firmly and with kindness, back to the point. Again, 'rounds' (p49) are a useful device to break this kind of pattern.

Occasionally - well, quite often -
some group leaders can encourage over-dependence

We all need to be needed. This is normal.

Sometimes though, a person's need to be needed gets out of proportion because his or her needs are not being adequately met. So that person strives to set up situations where they are needed by people who are themselves in need.

Some social workers, doctors, ministers of religion and people in the helping professions generally, fall into this category.

Some group leaders do too. This can mean that people in the group are not allowed to grow up emotionally. The leader, therefore, remains very much an immature source of wisdom, strength, help, comfort and so on.

A competent group leader allows members to grow in independence, including healthy disagreements and challenge.

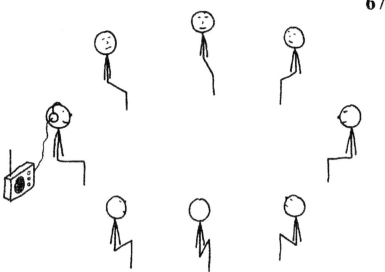

It is important to experience silences (planned or not) - however some members may find them difficult

Unplanned awkward silences can be very threatening for some people. They may want desperately to do something to break the silence, but are afraid that if they do, all eyes will turn upon them.

The leader should not jump in immediately to end the silence, either by ignoring it or talking about it. He or she should wait a little while and then ask what the silence is about, so that it can be talked through.

Some people may also find planned silences quite anxiety-making, especially if they are long. Others can enjoy such silences together, and find them helpful and moving.

So silences, planned or not, can affect members differently.

Anxiety is usually lessened if people know how long a planned silence is going to be.

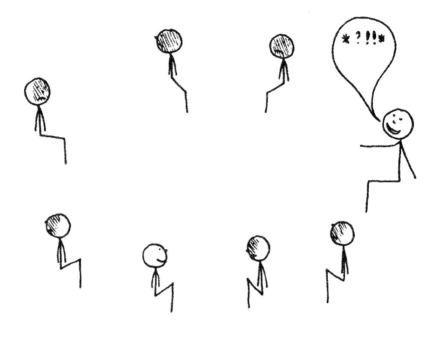

**For some reason
the subject of sex and sexuality seems to be avoided**

When we are in a group (as anywhere else), there is no hiding the fact that
we are either male or female. The difficulties which past generations have
had in discussing sex and sexuality are around today. Some people are more
inhibited than others.

Discussions about sex and sexuality will not arise in some groups because
their purpose is not orientated that way, but members still need to be aware
that each person present is showing a mixture of male and female character-
istics. However, it is not permissible to discuss sex in mixed groups in some
cultures, and such diversity must be respected.

**People often wait until the very last moment
before saying what's *really* on their mind**

It is well known by counsellors and therapists that a client will often wait until the session has nearly ended before talking about something that is worrying them, or which they feel diffident about revealing.

This is usually done because the client knows that if any upsetting emotions are aroused by this late 'revelation', he or she can make a quick exit because time is up!

The same thing happens in groups and the situation needs careful handling. A leader could fall into the trap of beginning the meeting all over again, so to speak, in order to look at what has been raised and not appear dismissive. This could lead to annoyance among those who wish to leave on time. So, when this group phenomenon arises the leader might suggest that the important matter is first on the agenda next time, as it needs to have the group's full attention.

Giving feedback

In some groups it may be appropriate for members to offer each other appraising comments to help develop their own performance. It is important, if such feedback is given, that the leader should define the rules for this and set an example. Feedback is helpful if it is:

- specific, eg: 'When you mentioned X in the group on Friday I found it useful.'
- personal, eg: 'When you keep interrupting Y I feel annoyed.'

Vague, impersonal statements which are not specific such as 'Everyone in the group thinks Z is a waste of time', are unlikely to enhance individual members or the life of the group.

Techniques such as asking each member in turn to state something appreciated or something regretted about the group, may be useful. Another possibility is for each member to think of a symbolic present they would like to give each fellow participant. For example, someone who contributes many new ideas may be symbolically offered a computer. The presents can also provide a gentle form of feedback, so long as they are sensitively offered, eg: a telephone for someone who doesn't keep in touch.

White elephants

Sometimes a person may reintroduce something which has previously arisen - they may even bring up the same thing repeatedly. Such 'white elephants' are particularly noticeable towards the end of the life of a group and are a rather puzzling symptom of the ending process. With experience, group leaders are not put off by this as it is 'normal'.

For example, a member may make repeated complaints about the same thing.

The bringing in of white elephants can be an indication of the group's value rather than otherwise.

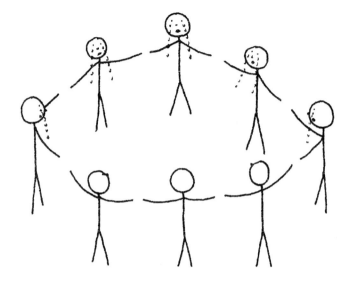

Some groups find it difficult to disband

Every group has a life of its own, and just as it was brought into being, so must it have an end.

Some groups, of course, meet for a continuing purpose and will go on year after year with changing membership.

Most groups, however, need a reasonable life span appropriate to their purpose. This avoids staleness, boredom and diminishing membership.

If people have formed good relationships during the life of the group, it is understandable that they won't want to break up. It is therefore essential that members have a chance to anticipate the coming feelings of loss, to share them, and to help each other in coming to terms with them. A party, games and small presents can help the process (like the symbolic ones on page 70 they should be sensitive).

Sometimes the party falls flat ...

There are occasions when there is too much unfinished business around to allow an end-of-group party to go with a swing.

A may still be seething at something **B** said five meetings ago.

C could be feeling hurt by a remark made by **D** last week.

E hasn't recovered from being made the group casualty two weeks ago.

F may feel that he or she just missed taking over the leadership. If only there had been a few more meetings .....

G may be cross with **D** for getting at **C**.

H may be the only one free of tangles and can't understand why people aren't enjoying themselves. (But if he or she can't understand then it looks as though there is some unfinished business here as well!)

74

Some groups can get too academic!

We want to acknowledge here the indirect help we have received from those who have written about groups and their workings, as well as the direct help from the leaders of courses, workshops and seminars we have attended over the years.

May your groups go well!

Bion, W (1990) *Experiences in Groups*, London, Routledge
Brown A (1992) *Groupwork*, Aldershot, Ashgate.
Kindred M & M (1998) *Once upon a group Exercises*, Southwell, 4M Publications
Maslow A (1984) *The Farther Reaches of Human Nature*, Harmondsworth, Penguin
Schutz, W C (1958) *A 3 Dimensional Theory of Interpersonal Orientation*, New York, Holt, Rinehart and Winston.
Schutz W C (1973) *Joy: Expanding Human Awareness*, Harmondsworth, Penguin
Vernelle, B (1994) *Understanding and Using Groups*, London, Whiting & Birch Ltd

Running a group - preparation checklist

Preparation for running a group is essential

Running a group may involve:

- starting one from scratch *or*

- taking over an existing group.

The checklist which follows relates to the former, but you can adapt it to the latter. For example, if you have been asked to take over an existing group, it would be wise to check that the purpose of the group is still clear to everyone, that the time and place of meetings are still convenient to members, and so on.

- **What is the exact purpose of the group?**

  *You need to make this clear to members.
  Clarity is the key to success.*

- **When will the group meet?**

  *Time, date, and number of meetings.
  Remember shift workers, people with children.*

- **Where will the group meet?**

  *Don't forget TDP (Time, Date and Place)
  and number of meetings must go on any
  notices to prospectiv members.*

- **Is the meeting place accessible to all?**

  *Are there any members with disability, either
  evident, eg: a person in a wheelchair, or
  hidden, eg: someone with a phobia about
  being on the upper floors of a high-rise building?*

- **What is the contract to be?**

   Will you keep to time boundaries?

  *Starting and finishing on time will mean
  that members know what to expect, and
  those who have commitments at the end
  of a meeting, such as getting back to
  take a babysitter home, will not be
  inconvenienced.*

What arrangements will you make about confidentiality?

*You need to agree with the members about what is for their ears only, and what may **never** be talked about outside the group. Unless this is established at the beginning and reinforced when necessary, members may be inhibited in what they say and do.*

 What feedback will be allowed to other people outside the group?

*This is not the same as confidentiality. The group may at times be working on something which, **for the time being**, needs to be kept within the group, so that it can be worked out properly.*

 Who will lead the group?

The person who does a lot of the preparation may not be the group leader and this needs to be clear to prospective members.

 Who will be responsible for which jobs?

There are some jobs which may not be the leader's responsibility, such as sending out notices and organising refreshments.

- **Will the meeting room be comfortable?**

    Consider temperature, ventilation, draughts, seating accommodation, lighting level.

- **What about audibility?**

    Some rooms may be too big and have an echo. One person in ten has some degree of hearing impairment.

- **If refreshments are to be served, what will they be?**

    Will food and drinks suit varying cultures and customs?

- **Is equipment in working order and are power points available?**

    Also check that audio and video tapes, software and the like will work satisfactorily on the equipment. Eg: 'Long play' videos will not work on a video recorder which only has the 'short play' facility. There is no substitute for rehearsal.

- **How will you handle lateness?**

    If anyone arrives late, it is better to continue with what the group is doing rather than stop to bring the latecomer up to date. The latter can be very frustrating for those who have arrived on time.

· **How will you deal with smoking?**

*It takes only one person smoking to spoil the atmosphere for any number of non-smokers. It is worth putting on the notices which go out to prospective members that there will be no smoking allowed, **or** that the issue will be discussed at the first meeting in order to arrive at a mutually satisfactory solution. (Some buildings and rooms have NO SMOKING notices anyway)*

· **How will you cope with on/off attendance?**

Groups work best when membership is stable and committed. You may need to state on the notices which go out to prospective members that members are expected to be committed to full attendance, and that they are to let the group know when absence is unavoidable.

• **Have you checked all materials?**

Have you made sufficient copies of any handouts? Have you made a list of what materials you need for each meeting?

• **Have you checked the 'messages' in your materials?**

- do they give a positive view of black people?
- do they convey the message that not everyone is slim, young and able-bodied?

80

*- do they convey the message that there are gay
and lesbian people as well as
heterosexuals?*
*- do they convey messages which place women
in an equal position with men?*

* **How will the ending of the group be recognised?**

*The ending of a group is just as important as
other parts of its life. Every ending is a loss,
with feelings of loss. Rituals are important -
see page 76 for suggestions.*